Jafta—The Town

Story by Hugh Lewin

Pictures by Lisa Kopper

Evans Brothers Limited London

My father met us, said Jafta,
when my mother and I went to town
for the funeral of one of my uncles.
My father worked in town and
it was so good to see him again.
He said it wasn't too far
to where he stayed.

There are more people in town,
you know, than ants in an ant-hill,
all going hurry hurry
and not talking to each other.

"Hold tight," said Father.
We would have been lost without him.
All the roads looked the same,
with motor-cars and lorries everywhere,
hooting and squealing like pigs.

It was also noisy in Father's room,
which he normally shared
with three other men
from the factory.
There aren't many birds
or singing crickets in town,
said Jafta.
In the streets there are more lights
than you'll see in a veld fire,
but you don't see the stars much.

I nearly got lost on the day of the funeral.
Mother said I was too young to go, so I was meant to stay inside.
But there were some children playing in the street
and I went to join them.

We played most of the afternoon.
The games were much the
same as at home.
We were in the middle of
hide-and-seek when I realised
I didn't know where I was.
I might have cried
if I hadn't been with
two boys who were
younger than me.

Then I saw Father and Mother coming back and I ran to them,
laughing, forgetting that they had been to a funeral.
But Father smiled, "Before a man is buried," he said,
"you must be quiet to honour him.
Afterwards, it's time to remember life
and be pleased that you are not dead too."
That night the adults had a big party.

Next day Father took us to the factory where he worked.

It was big and ugly. And the smell – ugh!

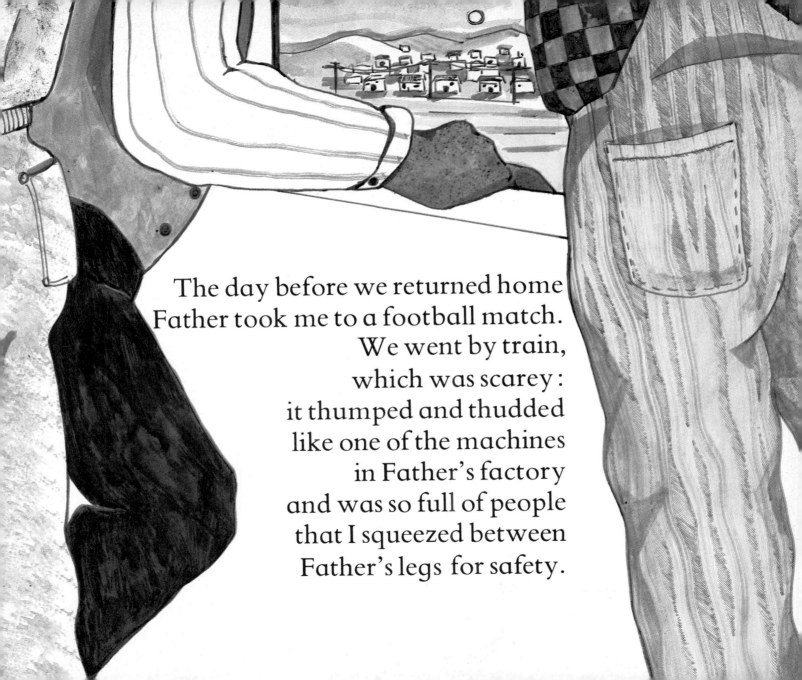

The day before we returned home
Father took me to a football match.
We went by train,
which was scarey:
it thumped and thudded
like one of the machines
in Father's factory
and was so full of people
that I squeezed between
Father's legs for safety.

At the football stadium, the noise was even louder, with shouting, chanting and singing.

Father carried me on his shoulders.
His team won and that was good.

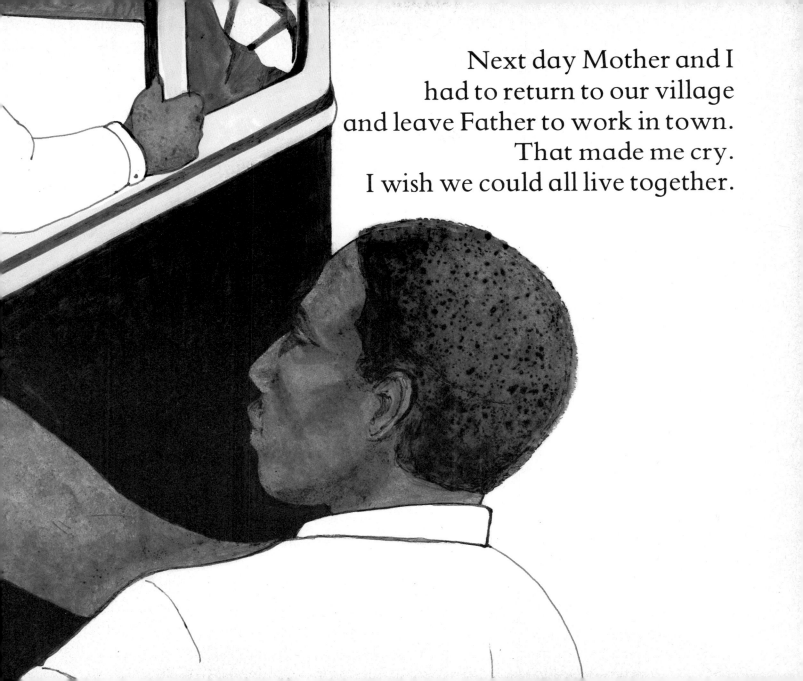

Next day Mother and I
had to return to our village
and leave Father to work in town.
That made me cry.
I wish we could all live together.

For Josie

First published 1983 by Evans Brothers Limited,
Montague House, Russell Square, London WC1B 5BX
Story © 1983 Hugh Lewin
Pictures © 1983 Lisa Kopper

British Library Cataloguing in Publication Data
Lewin, Hugh
Jafta—the town.—(Jafta's family series)
1. Children—Africa—Juvenile literature
2. Villages—Africa—Juvenile literature
3. Africa—Social life and customs—Juvenile
literature
I. Title   II. Kopper, Lisa
960'.09'734   DT14
ISBN 0–237–45677–X
NPR 205

Made and printed in Great Britain by
Purnell and Sons (Book Production) Limited
Paulton, Bristol